Awakening!
my journey within...

NISHI JUMNA

Balboa Press books may be ordered through booksellers or by contacting:

Balboa Press
A Division of Hay House
1663 Liberty Drive
Bloomington, IN 47403
www.balboapress.com
1 (877) 407-4847

ISBN: 978-1-5043-3294-1 (sc)
ISBN: 978-1-5043-3295-8 (e)

Library of Congress Control Number: 2015907705

Print information available on the last page.

Balboa Press rev. date: 8/17/2015

BALBOA
PRESS
A DIVISION OF HAY HOUSE

To Bram Jumna and Sheela Devi Jumna: my parents, my teachers, my first god and goddess, and my best friends.

Mum and Dad, I am eternally grateful for all that you have blessed me with. Your love and nurturing have allowed me to blossom into the woman I am. I love you.

Acknowledgments

It is often said that it takes a community to raise a child. Bringing a creative project such as this one to life is no different. It began with life events that moved me to transform and joyful memories that filled my heart with love and laughter. On this emotional continuum are many shades of emotions which color our lives and this book is a sampling of some of them. This journey began with the tender guidance and motivation of Brynn Saito, my creative writing instructor, who is a poet in her own right. Her encouragement sparked new avenues of exploration, which made me realize that there was more to me than I thought.

To Nithasha, Manesh, and Mahendra: my siblings, my confidants and my best friends. I miss you and love all that you represent in my life. You continue to be my teachers through the lives you live.

Finally, this acknowledgment would not be complete without my dear friend and colleague, Rev. Deborah Keizer, who inspired me to bring this book to print.

Thank you all for your part on this journey. Infinite gratitude and love to you all.

Contents

Birth of a Poet

The dictionary defines a poet as a person who has the gift of poetic thought, imagination, and creativity; expressed with the eloquence and sophistication. Reading this definition makes a poet seem like an extraordinary person with gifts of creativity privy to a few. Looking at these lines makes me wonder if I will ever have what it takes to be called a poet, or a writer for that matter.

I have studied the works of many such talented individuals and have marveled
at the creativity of others, yet I never considered myself to be one of them.
Perhaps, my style and drive germinates from my vision of the world.

Poetry is a means for my thoughts to come to life and to express
how I am moved by a situation, person, or subject.

Over the years I have dabbled in the possibility of writing. Some of my creations come relatively easily, and others need more nudging before they spill forth onto the paper; however, they eventually take form. The creative process of bringing my thoughts and emotions to life is one I am becoming more open to. In my earlier writings, I seemed more conservative in my choice of words and emotions. Naturally, my emotions lay buried in the text, dormant.

Embarking on this journey has been a catalyst to my creative process. The comfort of sharing details about myself among a group of open-minded and talented individuals has made expression a necessity rather that a process. In an environment where I feel safe, encouraged, and empowered, I find an eruption of zeal to not only create but to explore who I am.

Growing up in a foreign country and not being able to taste the richness of true Indian culture made me angry at first. I had difficulty seeing Africa as my home.

Immigrating to America has put a lot into perspective for me. My spiritual connections and the love of family are the foundation of my success. If I have these two components that sustain a wholesome life, I truly have it all. America gave me a new appreciation for the gifts I have been blessed with as well as a new perspective on life. With this appreciation came a voice to express the gratitude and bounty I feel for the blessings I have.

As I journey deeper into my core with each progressive exploration, there is a new me emerging. It's a paradoxical process of fear, trepidation, and one of infinite beauty. I am growing to love the new me and all the amazing things I am capable of creating. As the metamorphosis continues, my poetic expression evolves.

Poetry is a means to bring out what is blocking my flow in life: that nagging thought, that bubbling enthusiasm, the joy of friends, the sorrows of loss, the bravery of being bold, the disappointment of being jilted, and the courage to stand up for what I believe in. All these are the gifts of this miracle called life, and through poetry I found a vista for sharing my adventure.

In this sampling of my work, I have given you a palate of emotions. Life has its ups and downs, and I have tried to find myself in each one of these creations.

When I look at my work, there are a few things that come to mind. First, it's an expression of my emotions surrounding an event and how I am impacted by the event. However, there is more to my work than meets the eye. Embedded in these syllables are lessons, morals, themes, and an invitation to explore one's own emotions/biases about the topics.

Some of the themes that run through my poems are love, grief, surprise, appearance versus reality, loss, denial, separation, joy, confusion, appreciation, gratitude, sacrifice, emotional security, and acceptance. I am sure you will find more.

Themes are the threads that weave the tapestry. It's the blood that pulses through the veins of the poems. Appreciation of the themes is a unique and individualized experience that is tinted by ethnography and values. The same can be said for the interpretation and meaning of a poem. Acknowledging that the theme exists sets the stage for perception and imagination. In each of our minds, themes have the ability to conjure up scenes shaded by our morals, values, and experiences.

Let's trace our steps back to the interpretation and meaning of the poem. We have physical, mental, and spiritual bodies. Similarly, the poet's intent is irrelevant because every poem is a creation that has a figurative body camouflaged by the literal body that is influenced by the reader's perception.

The finite literal body of a poem delivers the concrete message about what I am expressing from within myself; however, the figurative or implied meanings are as infinite as there are stars in a galaxy.

This process, which I call creativity, holds the key to doors within myself that I did not know existed.

This path of self-discovery through creative expression is therapeutic on multiple levels. Personally, this path is an integration of parts of myself that are new to me as well as old habits and patterns, which I see in a new light. I discover more of who I am and who I can be. This process is redefining my purpose and opening me up to new possibilities. For this, I am grateful.

Now that you know more about me and how this process of creativity impacts me as an individual, let's go on to my work and play with what these poems mean to you.

Home Away from Home

Raped of my innocence by sons of another, in search of their future bountiful and bright,

I long for my children, torn from their mother under the cover of night.

My womb, pregnant with foreign rule, bears the progeny of dictators that plunder and fool.

Oh! My children, I feel your tears as you mourn.

A mother held captive, I am helpless, vulnerable, and torn.

Barren and dry, I long for love, to love, and be loved.

A daughter of India, born in Africa,

I deny my heritage and pledge my kinship to a mother I have never known.

Nurtured and supported by Africa's grace,

My disloyalty makes me lose face.

Enslaved like the mother by the rules of another,

I fail to see that Africa is my mother.

Barren and dry, I long for love, to love, and be loved.

Ungrateful for her blessings, I venture in search of foreign treasures.

Repeating the tragedy of her sons past, I abandon her for personal pleasures.

Traveling to the forbidden land of her lost sons, I turn my back on her, abandoned again.

Grateful for this pain disguised as opportunity, I bring tears to a heart already strained.

Looking back, I feel her pain searing in me …

For these pleasures I seek cannot compare with my mother's love.

Admiring her from afar, I long for her embrace as gentle as a dove.

Barren and dry, I long for love, to love, and be loved.

Mother Africa, my teacher in life,

Lead me home to your bosom to end this strife.

For wrongs can be righted

And mothers delighted

At the love of her children, awakened and enlightened.

No longer barren but lush with love, Mother Africa ...

You are loved,

You share love.

You eternally embody love in all its personification.

The Light in Me

Deep within, where the light once shone,

I feel this void from which the light has gone.

Filled with emotions of a burdensome nature,

I roam the park in search for closure.

There, on the park bench I sit,

Waiting patiently for the lamps to be lit.

They spiral, these emotions, they do!

As I sit in solace, releasing the slew,

They emerge; they challenge; and then they just drop

As I sit patiently allowing this flow that can't be stopped.

I notice that light in the distance.

My light.

It's back in me.

My light, that beacon of causeless happiness.

My reward for self-forgiveness.

Girl in the Wind

The August sun sets down to rest.

Exploring birds lay down to nest.

In the valley, an isolated log cabin sits secluded on the sandy bank,

Cloaked by the trees from the light of the sun.

Clouds of smoke curl out the chimney.

The evening breeze rustles through the leaves, whispering …

Branches sway to the melancholy waltz of trees.

The passing brook gurgles over the round pebbles.

A pleasurable, tranquil sight,

Deceiving me into believing this is where calmness broods.

The high-pitched cry escapes the walls of the cabin,

Breaching the silence, shattering it like breaking glass.

Nature cannot conceal such pain.

She feels what I feel.

As if by instinct, the speed of the breeze rises within the trees.

The leaves are curious, craning on the branches.

The snap of a branch heralds a human launch.

The door slammed shut where stillness once stood.

A sobbing maiden takes off into the woods,

Tears burning as they well up in her emotional eyes and roll down her

Dust-kissed cheeks.

Like a brook through the valley, the tears engrave a path down her face.

Blindly, she runs seeking shelter,

A place of safety, a place to hide.

She stumbles on a rock, undeterred.

Escape she must, and escape she will.

Against the wind she struggles, a lonely soul doing battle.

In circles she runs until solace is found.

Our girl in the wind, troubled and bound.

Predatory Fangs

Strengthening movements for racial justice, economic equity, and human rights.

Our birthright a gift from God,

Stolen from one of his creations from his kin of a lighter skin.

Snatched from their beds under the cover of night,

Children torn from parents, husbands from wives, and daughters from womanhood.

Under the innocent sky, dreams turn into nightmares.

No one is immune.

Black, Hispanic, Japanese, Indian:

Tainted fangs of prejudice.

Hungry, flesh-tearing fangs,

Ripping flesh from the skeleton of our community.

We can run, but we can't hide.

From the wilderness of Africa to the rice fields of Japan, from ancient Mexico to sacred India,

Our greatest loss is

The closing of the progressive mind.

Tino, My Precious Puppy

The shrieking howl of a lonely puppy pierces the night sky,

Banishing the heavenly sleep from my needy eyes.

Out of bed I drag myself reluctantly

Only to find the howler waiting expectantly.

The vigorous wag of his stunted tail shows his relief at the sight of me.

With a suppressed, shy whimper, he imparts,

"One more cuddle. Don't leave me, please."

This little bundle of fur with eyes of jet

Soft and furry, yet unpredictable and daring.

He brings joy immeasurable to the grief-laden hearts of those around him.

Tino is his name.

Destruction is his game.

Lotus Blossom (For Susan Mangel)

As the embodiment of harmony in nature, I rise as its regal daughter.

From the bowels of the earth,

My tuberous root sends my pedunculated throne through the muddy ripples of water,

High up into the air where I will make my debut as the fruit of growth and hope.

Earth, water, air, and fire come together to give me life.

In the sea of lush green leaves,

Hiding the ripples of the pond,

My throne rises high above the rest of the plants in competition for the love of the sun.

Cocooned in the calyx of septals, I ascend,

Waiting patiently and eagerly for a kiss from the sun.

Soon! Soon! It will be time. I am eager.

As morning approaches,

Dawn is breaking.

The sun stretches his arms to embrace the earth.

Over the mountains and through the clouds, he rises.

Golden rays kiss my septals, coaxing them to unfurl as I come to life.

One tender kiss after another, and I am lost in this beautiful waltz of light.

I blossom into a regal chalice,

A chalice full of radiant, blush pink, sun-kissed petals.

Straining against my peduncle,

I follow him across the sky.

This is a lifelong dance.

For soon, he will be gone.

I will retreat into my calyx in anticipation of yet another dance.

My soft, sweet petals tingle in response to his light.

The beauty of everything around me fades in his presence.

The water lilies chatter below me to get a glimpse of his handsomeness,

But it is I, the lotus blossom, on my queenly peduncle

Who is first to bat my coy petals at him in the morning light.

Looking Glass

I see before me an image in the looking glass.

Oh! What an illusion, what a farce.

A portrait of wholesome innocence and simplicity.

Sitting in the lotus position at the feet of our guru,

hanging onto his every word, I paint the picture of piety.

Nodding on cue as if I were really listening,

While my mind wrestled with the distractions of my heart.

This image blinds you to my true duplicity.

My mind is on the shore of the Pacific, where my true love is.

A married man!

Forbidden fruit!

The temptation is strong;

Resistance is weak.

The mirror to my thoughts are my eyes.

Behind them lie the dreams so devious I dare not voice.

I am what I want you to see, a pious devotee.

Hidden from you is the truth of my life, known only to me:

The devious adulteress who stole him from an eight-year-old.

My desire to please all the men and women in my life has entangled my spirit.

In each I see a trait or two that pleases me.

In the silence of secrecy, I enjoy these pleasures.

The warmth of true happiness I lack but treasure.

Forbidden fruit may taste of pleasure but suffocates the bearer with guilt and shame.

The tenderness and affection of loyalty is but a mirage in the desert;
      visible on the horizon but forever out of reach.

Tired and in need of loving, I return to my abode.

What do I name it?

My temple of joyous memories, my precious home,

Or a building devoid of feeling, a house of sand and stone.

Message from Ma

I want to tell you something …

Something truer than truth,

Something you doubt but feel deep in your core.

An emotion that lifts your lips to the heavens, knowing that which is truer than truth dwells within you.

Born of flesh, you are not kin,

Yet!

In spirit, we are one,

Merging as clouds do when they collide one into another.

There's no telling where one begins and the other ends.

Through eyeballs of ether, as transparent as flawless quartz,

I witness your smile and your tears, too.

As you go about your day-to-day life thinking I am not there,

I embrace you as tightly as a creeper hugs a tree trunk—this much is clear.

The bittersweet whispers hidden deep in your heart call to me with words unspoken.

Like gems in the limelight, they call with their sparkle.

Our bond is ancient yet new—

Ancient in the making, yet new to your perception.

These material senses keep you from me.

They have crippled your ability to recognize our cosmic form.

Yet!

My beautiful child, as lost as a needle in a haystack,

I have found you.

I am with you.

Oblivious to your material mind, you bask in my glory like a flower in the sun.

My beloved child,

I want to tell you something.

Something you will never hear, not with your ears you won't.

Something I want to tell you that's heard with your heart …

As the wind sings through the trees and the waves to the shore,

I sing to you …

I love you.

Letter to Lotus Blossom

Sitting on the bank of the pond, I look at all the beauty that surrounds you.

How fortunate you are to be the most beautiful blossom of them all.

The lilies and roses pale in comparison to your delicate charm.

Your sun-kissed petals unfurl at the break of dawn; the garden rises to the occasion of your awakening.

The bees are buzzing around, waiting for a taste of you as you tilt your crown to face the sun.

The birds are chirping and hopping from leaf to leaf in celebration.

Your stalk rocks you gently in the morning breeze.

The soft fragrance of elegance surrounds you as the day gets brighter.

Of course, you're oblivious to my presence, for you only have eyes for the sun.

I wonder if you noticed the scent of the roses or the eagerness of the
hummingbirds as they frolicked in the foliage around you.

The ferns are hanging off the trees to get a glimpse of you as the willow on
the far end of the pond sways to the beat of your waltz with the sun.

The adjoining orchard patch beckons with the sweet smell of oranges, but you only have eyes for the sun.

Oh lotus blossom! Your sights are set too high. For in your quest to love
the sun, you have missed the love that surrounds you.

The Courage to Love

The green fists of the peonies

Break my heart.

The sun strokes them.

They open

Into the curls,

Taking it away

Under the shifty wind.

The great wedding,

Flowers,

Fluttering in the air

Gladly and lightly,

Beauty!

Brave!

Do you love this world?

Half-dressed and barefoot,

Exclaiming their dearness

To be wild and perfect for a moment.

Passing Winds

Step by step, I wander through the woods:

Through the path gallantly lined by aging oaks,

The music of the breeze whispering through the trees.

Dry leaves rustle their pain at my crushing feet,

Their rhythm as regular as my footsteps.

The birds are nesting, preparing for winter.

Here and there, the trees are balding.

The forest is dressed in a carpet of golden hues—reds, browns, oranges, yellows, and golds.

As far as the eye can see can, the horizon blends into the heavens.

The setting sun lays down to rest.

Her golden rays peek through the trees, creating pillars of brilliant light.

Oh! So serene is this sight.

A nearby tree bellows invitingly to me.

Climb me! Climb me!

It is a temptation I'm unable to resist.

Perched on a branch in mid-air,

I savor my surroundings, so colorful and fair.

The forest is silent;

The trees are still.

Waiting! Waiting, patiently.

For what, I can't imagine. What are we waiting for?

"Soon, dear one. Soon!"

Whispers the Great Oaks, knowingly.

My curiosity peaking, I look around from side to side.

What is it?

Where is it?

I don't see it.

Oh! Behold this beauty untold—

The mocking laughter of the rolling winds as she gushes from behind the hills.

Like a magic carpet, she cuts through the forest—

Over the treetops, around their trunks, scattering the fallen leaves into the air.

The branches of the trees sway frantically to and fro.

Peals of laughter escape through my vocal cords …

Such joy … so free … Fun! Fun! Fun!

Their leaves are everywhere, high and low.

Like confetti at a wedding,

The air is bejeweled with the warm hues of autumn.

The wind smiles naughtily to herself as she dodges the branches that try to trap her.

Free is she, for that's her nature.

Generous is she to the ones she loves,

Transient is her stay, like a passing dove.

The trees generously give their leaves to please her, for no sooner has she come,

She passes and is gone.

There is the unspoken promise of a reunion, of another encounter.

The forest is silent again,

A silence with a difference:

Not one of anticipation but one of satisfaction.

The passing winds have come and gone.

We have born the bliss of her company.

These memories of her we treasure until we next enjoy her pleasure.

Oh! Passing winds, whose presence our lives enchant,

Pass this way again.

Do us this humble pleasure.

As days roll into weeks and weeks into months,

With anticipation we watch the hills for your return.

Curtain of Tears

A melody hangs in the air around us.

The lyrics, so potent, dart toward my heart like iron filings to a magnet.

The magnet, so cold and emotionless.

My precious heart, fibrillating with turbulant feelings.

Vulnerable to these sweet, merciless words, which cause it to bleed with each vivid memory in my mind.

I look up and wonder.

Could a few words move a man to such emotion?

Through a curtain of salty tears, I see before me a reflection of my memories.

Bittersweet memories cloud my mind.

I am seated here before you, but my mind is racing to destinations far and wide.

How am I to hide my feelings?

My eyes are the mirror to my soul, and you can read me as clearly as a book.

Decisions! Decisions!

How is a woman to survive?

Some are simple, others complicated.

With each passing day, the knot in my throat grows tighter, and the air in my lungs grows thinner.

Oh merciful Lord, I pray

With the dawn of each new day, grant me the courage to fulfill my dreams.

As I sail through my difficulties on your wings to make the right choices,

Fill my heart with sunshine.

Make it so that the next time I look up through this curtain of tears,

My heart will be singing; my ears will be ringing.

In the rain, I will be dancing the dance of joy for a battle won.

My Pen Ran out of Ink, But I'm Writing for the Falling Rain

The world around me is deaf to the music of the rain.

The tempo of her raindrops mirrors the emotions of my soul.

Jagged bolts of lightning shatter the cloudy sky,

Inviting rolling doldrums of thunder in their wake.

The dykes of the heavens give way to torrential rains.

On a deserted street, I stand and bask in the glory of nature so grand.

Illuminated in the glow of a street lamp,

The diamond raindrops glitter in the smoky, gray sky,

Her anger unleashed upon this tainted earth.

With surging gushes, the land is sanctified.

She'll be gone when her work is done:

When the rivers are full and the atmosphere is saturated with the scent of the sodden earth.

When the sky is clear, and the stars twinkle bright.

When the grass stands tall, and my rain-drenched body is hugged by my cold, saturated clothes.

I smile to myself, frozen to the bone, yet warm in my heart.

How I love thee, torrential rains—

The freedom with which you fall, no boundaries at all.

The designer of my destiny,

The composer of my symphony

Old Faithful

My heart aches with longing as I reminisce about the memories we've made.

My escort to the bus stop on cold winter mornings.

Chasing the postman and the passersby on the street.

Protective canine friend.

The vigorous wag of your tail when the kitchen door opens in the morning, expressing your joy.

The way you jump up with joy when you're anxious to grab a titbit from my hand.

Those huge brown eyes haunt my sleeping hours.

To the very last moment of your life on Earth, you trusted our ability to care for you.

To do what was best for you.

Thinking of your last waking moments brings tears to my eyes and a knot in my throat.

I still wonder whether that was the best decision.

The sight of those trusting brown irises, branded eternally in my mind

Do you miss us as much as we miss you?

Thoughts of you make my heart weep with joy.

The fun we shared is now a distant memory replaced with grief for our loss.

Your absence has created a void.

Our precious Bingo, we love you eternally.

Haiku

Migraine

White light! Piercing shards!
Blurred vision! Shattering pain!
My exploding head!

Traffic

Impatient drivers
Hurrying at a snail's pace,
Getting nowhere fast.

Full Moon

Radiant lunar!
Pregnant possibility!
Goddess's blessings.

Guru

Bow in surrender
Opening to divine grace
Epic redemption.

Wind

Whistling through trees,
Carrying seed to the womb,
Invisible power.

Rain

Angry clouds converge,
Raindrops pelting arid sand.
Saturated! Peace!

Food

Curious nostrils,
Salivating taste buds,
Spicy adventure.

Bhaiya! (Brother)

Texting maniac.
Infectious, radiant smile.
My heart is stolen.

Mia (Tash's Husky)

Loyal furry friend,
Doll's eyes of fake innocence,
Tail wagging mayhem.

Kali Ma

Dark Mother of time,
Churning wombs of creation,
Bloodless sacrifice.

Love

Chasing emotions,
Foggy communication,
Unrequited love!

Twin Flames

Single, ancient soul.
Divided in lovers apart.
Destined to unite.

New Moon

Waxing crescent,
Opening cosmic doors,
Twilight jewel.

Shiva and Shakti

Cosmic creators
Powerfully passionate,
Manifesting life.

Mother

Gift of genes most fair
Embraced in her love, most pure.
Eternally mine!

Shakti

Shakti!

The universe manifests the wife of Shiva.

Queen!

Endowed with unlimited power.

Her position?

Evokes a series of questions.

Shakti!

Vibrant! Active force!

Content of all terms:

Knowledge, unmanifest cosmic energy, illusion.

Samaya:

The secret meaning of mantra.

Feminine gender.

Transcendental reality.

The knower of the secret meaning of mantra.

Shakti!

There is only one.

Force

Force!

Active or dormant?

Light, delight, and beauty!

Characteristics of Kali.

Force!

Expressed or impeded?

Divisions of discipline:

Overpowering influence on others.

Most prominent,

It's well defined

Within its fold.

Emphatically claims its association,

Developed sophisticated philosophy

With considerable ambiguity.

Traditional adherents,

Both ancient and modern,

Attempt to demonstrate

How to worship.

Concepts relate.

Authenticity!

Interpreting one's own etymology.

The Power Within

Women!
The same issues—
More begin to awaken.
Feminist movements,
Supportive female friends.
Help her learn. Enable her.
Always seen as "Adam's rib."
Vitality and power from man.
Loathsome!
Transpose to transpersonal form
Beyond concrete thinking—
Another layer of meaning
Materialized on a biological level
Realized on a spiritual.
Her imagination and dreams,
Transpersonal beginnings,
Experience the Goddess.
Woman!
Play into existence.
Pretty incredible performance.

For the Love of the Goddess

To complain, plead, lament.

Tearful confessions

Great Goddess, far away.

Each individual, a personal goddess.

Who would hear her prayer?

Private devotion

With her priestess.

Sacrifices offered,

Libations of wine,

New Moon feast,

Ceremony of the reigning queen.

Fertility of the soil,

Fecundity of the womb.

Holy ceremony,

Mystical practices,

Bloom and blossom again.

Resurrection, a reunion.

Celebrated ceremony,

Music and song.

Sacred marriage,

Myth and ritual.

A profound union.

The Journey Home

From my mother's womb,
The journey begins;
No destination in sight.
Guided from within,
My cherished birthright.
Through obstacles and hurdles I navigate,
Mesmerized by Maya
To believe I am this body.

Lead by my soul
To allow all that is whole
From shadow to light, I contemplate
The process of my birthright.

The Price of Beauty

Weaving through traffic,

Hasty to be on time.

Perceived emergency of a fickle mind.

Olfactory assault!

Peroxide fumes!

Fake color!

Potent concoctions!

Financial burden, considered necessary.

Patient endurance,

Caustic procedure.

Drastic measures, defying aging.

Graceful life process, avoided like the plague.

First world feminine insanity.

Grief

My mother,

She died!

My mother,

She was pleased

To hear me laugh.

"I want to know," she said, "that you are getting along."

This was her way of saying, comfort each other.

It was hard to be together, Dad and me.

Yet, our shared loss

Drew us closer.

For the first time, Dad was able to cry,

A special gift.

My mother was there to help me

Sort my feelings of love and abandonment.

The story of mom's dying,

So calm.

I sense her words came from a source outside herself.

It comforted me to think, *Mum was home*.

Nature

Mystery!

Larger experience!

Challenging worldviews!

Discover their gifts.

The importance of nature.

Rocks so beautiful,

Each one unique from the ocean floor.

Ecstatic insights that come unexpectedly.

Caught outdoors, a woman made love for the first time.

Astonished eroticism.

The serenity of a lake at sunrise.

Memories that calm.

My own unconscious filters keep me from understanding her importance.

Passion, full of emotions.

The union of human and Earth.

From deep within my bones,

Heart of Nature beckons.

Inspired, I am learning

From the elements to the seasons

And stages of human development.

Nature is an experience of holistic perception—

Relieved, engaged, and curious.

I am one with the Earth.

Shifting paradigms from linear to natural.

Serve the Earth;

Let the beauty we love fill us.

Appreciation, longing, and understanding that we belong to each other.

Sitting under the stars.

Meeting in the wilderness at dawn.

Universe offering us a rite of passage.

Crossing the threshold into sacred time,

Returning to life with gifts anew.

A ceremony of reverence when hearts can fully open to the wonder of nature.

Falling in Love

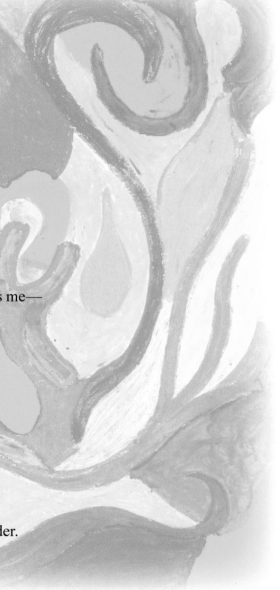

Self-blaming to avoid a relationship.

Found "the one" over and over again.

Feeling hopeless!

Giving up!

Secretly hoping and waiting …

Romantic fantasy.

Waiting for a mirage.

Fear and limitations, overwhelming!

Warrior Goddess, awaken in me.

Free my heart to feel the love within.

Free my heart to make me whole.

Opening to the understanding of the truth that is me—

Nothing can hurt me.

I need nothing to complete me.

I am one with spirit, which is me.

I choose my relationship, devoid of fear.

Unconditional self-love,

Finding what serves me best.

My heart won't be broken.

My heart won't be hurt.

This journey of opening my heart wider and wider.

Nourished on compassion and self-love.

No longer overwhelmed and scared.

Warrior Goddess, I am prepared.

I'm over my whining.

I can do this.

There's a lot going on that I can't handle.

It's going to be okay.

I am here with you,

From this place of loving.

I am good to go.

I am the Warrior Goddess.

I have fallen in love with me!

The Mystery of Dance

The mystery of dance, inviting on this spring night.

Friends, music, moonlight, and the sweet scent of jasmine.

The perfect combination.

I give myself over.

The experience is sheer pleasure.

My mind is quiet;

I experience the bliss;

I let go.

Totally immersed in sensation.

For the first time in a long time

I perceive the oneness, the peace and this connection to the whole.

Fountain of knowledge,

Fountain of truth,

Fountain of sensual pleasure,

I reconnect with my entire being.

The mystery of dance, finds me

Seeking creative expression.

Mesmerized in the movement,

Emerging desires.

Healthier relations with myself,

The birthing of a fierce new awareness.

I am one with this whole.

A portal of interrelatedness.

My paradigm is shifting,

Emerging from my beliefs to savor the new.

I am awake.

I am dancing.

The mystery unfolds but is far from solved.

Matrophobia

Matrophobia!

"Just like her,"

Surrounded with despair,

Rife among women,

Doing things as our mothers did,

The same attitudes,

The identical responses.

I hear my mother's words escape through my lips.

Her tone resonates through my chest.

"But this isn't me."

It's just like her,

My mother!

I have turned into to her,

Haven't I?

Physically exorcised,

Emotionally embodied.

I am "just like *her*."

Pilgrimage

A place inside

Comes to life,

Patterns repeated.

Images!

Women carrying offerings.

Locate the shrine!

Discover together.

I don't know everything.

We proceed.

Untranslated hieroglyphics.

Perhaps a priestess descended these steps before us.

Our journey continues.

Rituals performed close to the sea.

A woman pouring libations.

Ritual at the crown of sacred feminine.

We found the shrine.

We inaugurated it.

Our sacred tradition.

Placing offerings on ancient stone,

Ritual begun.

Women's sacred place of birth and renewal.

In this ritual we return the gift of life to Earth,

Our connection to ancient women.

Our connection to divine feminine.

Taste the sweetness pilgrims take home.

Dreams

In this form,

Which allows the imagination to be active,

What does it make me think about, want, and feel?

Sometimes I wake up knowing.

It just pops.

Other times it takes work.

It takes thought.

Embodying the dream …

That's what it's about.

The characters and objects

I am wanting to understand—

I let them speak through me.

Become me.

Bringing the dream into my body.

Dreamer becomes one with the dream.

What is inconceivable becomes forgivable.

One with our unconscious, we complete our dream,

Find solace and peace.

It is healing, heart opening.

A visceral understanding of compassion

Flowing from me.

The deep truth of dreams liberating me from the shackle of the unconscious.

Feelings of hope,

Feelings of fear,

Feelings of love,

Feelings of pain,

The collage of reality buried in my dream.

Sexuality

Flower of rebirth,

Phallic likeness.

Rebirth and sexuality

Charmed,

Immune to the laws.

To steal me

Craves power,

Understand her nature,

Insisting on equality.

She refuses to copulate

Outside relationship or regulation,

Possessed by insatiable sexuality.

Sexually, lawless creature

Outside the bounds of community.

Unexpressed fears,

Desires named,

She wanted womanhood to be deserving.

Let go of it.

Dissolved in tears,

The realization of her own dark craving.

Resistance weakens.

She is prepared.

Another state of awareness dawns.

Reiki Healing

Seeing psychically,
Knowing with the body,
Feeling a visual image,
I know that feels right.
Hands-on healing,
The blood speaks through channels of energy,
Systems of understanding
Passed along in healing tradition.
Contemporary body workers
Healing through my body,
Listening to these messages,
Observing the body.
Energy registers.
Hands on,
Healing begun.
Amazing!
Intense phenomena!
Incredible!
Deep moving forces of light.
Erupting esoteric wisdom.

Relations with Cuba

Violating "territorial integrity."
Lawmakers quick to criticize
"Trading convicted criminals"
Invites dictatorial, rogue regimes.
Using Americans as bargaining chips.
Further human rights,
Democracy in Cuba.
Respect your passion.
Share your commitment.
Liberty and democracy.
Illusion continued,
Barriers to freedom
Bring about transformation.
End outdated approach
Begin a new chapter.

Death by Firing Squad

Charges of conspiracy to commit mutiny,

Militants sit handcuffed.

All pled not guilty.

    Sentenced to death,

    A "genocidal verdict."

    Journalists barred from the trial

    By military authorities.

    Wasting lives of innocent soldiers

    Without any legal justification.

    Commended for their bravery,

    Sacrifice for inexplicable reasons,

    Charged with mutiny.

Cowardice for refusing to fight the extremists.

The Love of a Nurse

From our stations,

Taking in the sounds and smells.

Patients around us.

Soft, hissing lulls of artificial breathing.

Mechanical chirps of cardiac monitors.

Amid this attempt to sustain life are huddles of families.

Whispered voices around the beds.

The power of the human condition.

Cramped rooms full of machines and prayers.

I am welcome here.

Families cling to hope and prayer.

One complication after another threatens the hope they hold onto,

Laughter despite challenges.

Fear hidden behind bright smiles.

Regardless of outcome,

The love follows them.

A piece of it stays with me

As our stories go their separate ways.

Forever changed.

Love lives on.

Waiting for Death to Arrive

In the dimly lit hospital room,

Surrounded by family saying their final good-byes,

The lifeless one lies waiting …

Confined to this bed by invisible restraints of dis-ease.

Life-sustaining processes come to a screeching halt.

Supported mechanically, the heaving ventilator forces a rebellious chest to rise,

Each breath more artificial than the last.

Life's mocking paradox.

You can feel him in the air …

Heavy, cold, detached.

Departure is around the corner … we wait in agony.

Staccato heart holds on reluctantly.

Further and further apart, the contractions spread as we approach the gate.

One little green dot bouncing across the bedside monitor is the only sign of life.

Beep! Beep! Beep!

The lively dot growing weary and tired.

Giving in a little more with each beat, growing further apart.

Surrendering to the process.

Ready to make his final journey home.

Among hushed sobs and burdened hearts,

Warm hands wrap tenderly around a cold frail one.

His muscles have lost their will to grasp.

The time has come.

The flat green line is the only sign

This physical life is done.

Fooled by the Queen

Gifted by a friend,

She stands regally on my altar,

This unidentified queen of the heavens.

Welcomed by the pantheon of Hindu goddesses who tower over her.

She holds her ground with grace and power.

Voluptuous in her form,

Naked as the day she was born.

Her beauty challenges social norms.

From breasts like melons, so full and ripe,

To broad, orgasmic hips for pleasure by night.

Her alabaster skin glistens in the dancing candlelight,

Tempting the will of men by day and night.

Synonymous with Venus, most lovable and fair

Thief of the Me, from her father's lair,

The goddess of heaven ventures below.

Stripped of her lapis, she is transformed.

Resurrected from a corpse on a peg, she ascends.

Equally cunning as she is loving.

The Earth Mother

An artistic expression

Inspired by her grace,

Muddy finger pinching and smoothing

Mounds of clay, molded into her resemblance.

A figment of a student's imagination.

Conjured in meditation.

Manifested through the intuitive flow of the artist's hand,

The mother of creation takes shape in physical form.

A catalyst to spiritual awakening.

Infused with mantra, she emerges slowly.

Souls connect, that of goddess and child.

Eyes of onyx, heart of rhodocrosite—

Compassion and empathy, intentions ignite.

The power of femininity.

Sacred ritual and song.

Celebrations!

Mother is born!

Who Decides?

A woman's body,

The seat of creation.

Temple of the chalice,

Epicenter of procreation.

A social commodity to religious bigots,

Imposing patriarchal decisions over her right to decide.

The issue of contraception …

A judicial battle over who decides.

The sacred feminine who within resides

Or capitalist hypocrites who threaten poverty and strife.

Consummated within marriage, the fruit of sacred union.

Yet, anywhere else, just an act of lust and passion.

Needs fulfilled without consequences …

Preventing the birth of a bastard child.

Contraception …

A woman's right over her body and her life.

Futility of the Game

Royal dancer in lotus pose.

Serene meditation ...

Sitting still in cosmic awareness,

Processing the material matrix:

Power and grace,

Her mystic glamor.

Harnessing divine will to support humanity

Observing the dilemma of troubled mankind

The heavenly mother, ready to respond.

Accepting my offering in chaliced palms.

Fragile blossoms for my twin flame.

Distant in space, Siamese of my soul.

Offerings to the Mother, a token celebrating our ordeal.

Fragile as the petals,

Fragrant and sweet.

Cloaked in words harsh and tender.

Emotions vague,

Behaviors confusing.

Shrouded in veils of social conformity.

Spiritual destiny postponed.

Our passion suffocated by ego before it is born.

What I Want

(Message from a friend)

I want to feel secure.

I want to feel valued.

I want to feel loved.

I want to consistently feel this for myself.

I want to feel nurtured.

I want to feel peace.

I want to manifest my desires.

I want people to see divinity in each other.

I want to be strong.

I want to be able to stand up for what I value.

I want to take care of myself consistently.

I want to see divinity in everyone.

I want to appreciate how I see the world.

I want to see value in spirituality.

I want to live the teachings.

I want everyone to see the beauty I see.

I want them to taste the nectar of human relations.

I want to take care of myself consistently.

Shiva!

Shiva! Shiva! Shiva! Shambho!

Ash smeared, hide clad, titan of Kashi.

Destroyer of the trilogy.

Absolute consciousness.

Choreographer of the Tandava!

Disowned by King Daksha.

Husband of Sati!

Doting consort.

Personified by the lingam.

Adventurous!

Courageous!

Daring!

Fearless!

Eleventh incarnation as dutiful Hanuman.

Heavenly monkey with a spiritual agenda.

Devout servant of Lord Rama,

Savior of Ma Sita,

Arsonist of Lanka.

Roles differ, incarnations transform with evolution.

His rugged sensuality palpable in every form.

Love his deviance!

Savor his passion!

Embrace his arrogance!

Lovably defiant!

Shiva! Shiva! Om Namah Shivaya!

Kaashi Vishwaanaatha Gange! (He who lives on the banks of the Ganges River at Kaashi.)

My King of Wands

I've spent my entire life dreaming of you.

It has been so long; I truly believed that you were a figment of my imagination,

A figment, stuck in my mind with no way out.

I adored you from afar and looked for you in every man I met.

They always fell short of my King of wands.

Not enough personality, too fickle, too materialistic, and not spiritual enough …

The list goes on …

My King of Wands, my partner in spirit and in tarot.

Trapped in a deck foretelling the future.

My King of Wands, you are perfect in every way.

Every component of you in just the right proportions to complement me.

My twin flame, manifested in the flesh.

Your smile, your humor, your commitment to us, your free spirit,

Your sense of humor, your protective caring …

Where you are weak, I am strong.

Where I am tarnished, you shine.

Where I lack, you are abundant.

My cosmic complement.

Like pieces of a puzzle we fit like hand in glove.

Your queen is delighted to see her king in the flesh …

Life just got happier and my heart brighter, for you are near.

No longer trapped in my mind, or in a picture on a card,

But alive in my mind, my heart, and every pore of my being.

Huggable, loveable, air breathing body of love …
Our joyful lives dedicated to one another
On the runway destined to a lifelong adventure
Of loving friendship.
Welcome home, my royal highness.

Printed in the United States
By Bookmasters